iScience
Science in the Real World

Trees

by Emily Sohn and Karen J. Rothbardt

NORWOODHOUSE PRESS
Chicago, Illinois

Norwood House Press
Chicago, Illinois

For information regarding Norwood House Press, please visit our website at
www.norwoodhousepress.com or call 866-565-2900.

Contributor: Edward Rock, Project Content Consultant

Editor: Lauren Dupuis-Perez

Designer: Sara Radka

Fact Checker: Sam Rhodes

Photo Credits in this revised edition include: Getty Images: Artur Debat, 4, Westend61,
12; Pixabay, Byunilho, background (paper texture), GDJ, background (tech pattern);
Shutterstock: Anna Om, cover, 1, Tommy Lee Walker, 11, Rob Crandall, 17, Halfpoint, 16

Library of Congress Cataloging-in-Publication Data

Names: Sohn, Emily, author. | Rothbardt, Karen, author. | Sohn, Emily. iScience.
Title: Trees / by Emily Sohn and Karen J. Rothbardt.
Description: [2019 edition]. | Chicago, Illinois : Norwood House Press, [2019] | Series: iScience
  | Audience: K to grade 3. | Includes bibliographical references and index.
Identifiers: LCCN 2018057833 | ISBN 9781684509652 (hardcover) |
  ISBN 9781684043651 (pbk.) | ISBN 9781684043767 (ebook)
Subjects: LCSH: Trees—Juvenile literature.
Classification: LCC QK475.8 .S64 2019 | DDC 582.16—dc23
LC record available at https://lccn.loc.gov/2018057833

Hardcover ISBN: 978-1-68450-965-2
Paperback ISBN: 978-1-68404-365-1

Contents

iScience Puzzle 6

Discover Activity 8

How Can You Describe Trees? 9

What Do Trees Need? 12

What Can Hurt Trees? 13

Why Do Trees Have Roots? 14

How Does a Tree Grow? 15

Science at Work 16

Connecting to History 17

Solve the iScience Puzzle 19

Beyond the Puzzle 21

Glossary 22

Further Reading/Additional Notes 23

Index 24

Note to Caregivers:
In this updated and revised iScience series, each book poses many questions to the reader. Some are open ended and ask what the reader thinks. Discuss these questions with your child and guide him or her in thinking through the possible answers and outcomes. There are also questions posed which have a specific answer. Encourage your child to read through the text to determine the correct answer. Most importantly, throughout the book, encourage answers using critical thinking skills and imagination. In the back of the book you will find answers to these questions, along with additional resources to help support you as you share the book with your child.

Words that are **bolded** are defined in the glossary in the back of the book.

What Are Trees Like?

Trees are like little worlds. Animals live in them. Plants grow on top of them. Look closely at a tree. You'll see a lot more than just leaves and branches.

There's a whole lot going on in there!

Which Tree Is Right for Your Tree House?

You and your friend want a tree house in the woods. You need to decide which tree will be best to build it in. In this wooded area, there are four types of trees: oaks, willows, maples, and pines. Which tree will you choose?

Choice 1: Oak Tree

Choice 2: Willow Tree

Choice 3: Maple Tree   Choice 4: Pine Tree

Here are some things to think about:

1. Is the tree strong enough to hold your tree house?

2. Does the tree have a good shape to fit a tree house?

3. Do insects live in this kind of tree? What else might make this tree a bad place to stay in?

4. Does the tree drop nuts, fruits, or even branches?

What Are the Parts of a Tree?

Which is the best tree to put your tree house in? To find out, grab a pencil and a notebook. Now, go outside. Find a park or a street with trees on it. Draw as many of the trees as you can.

Now, look at your pictures. How are the trees alike? How are they different? Where would you put a tree house in each one?

You know a tree when you see one. That's because all trees share some things in common. Here are some parts that every tree has: leaves, branches, a trunk, and **roots**. How else are trees alike?

◆ parts of a tree

◆ Different parts of a tree help it to grow and thrive.

How Can You Describe Trees?

Trees are like people. No two are exactly the same. Oak and maple trees have wide leaves. They also have thick, stiff branches. But willow trees have thin leaves. They also have thin, bendy branches.

Would you rather climb an oak tree or a willow tree? Remember: You will have to climb a tree to build a house in it.

What Do Trees Do?

Some trees drop all of their leaves every fall. Oaks, maples, birches, and willows are types of trees that do this.

Why do you think leaves fall off some trees? Do leaves drop off where you live? If so, when do they do it? When do they grow back?

Some trees keep their leaves all year. Pine trees, spruce trees, and fir trees all do this. These trees have **needles**. Needles are narrow leaves.

◆ Some trees lose their leaves for winter. Some trees keep their leaves all year long.

Do you want to put your tree house in a tree that loses its leaves? Why or why not?

Some trees grow fruits or nuts. Apples and cherries are fruits that grow on trees. Pecans and almonds are nuts that grow on trees. Acorns are nuts that grow on oak trees.

◆ Apples could hurt if they fell on you!

Where do fruits and nuts end up when they fall? What happens if they fall on people? On cars? On streets? Do you want your tree to have fruit or acorns on it?

What Do Trees Need?

Trees are plants. All plants are living things. They need sunlight and air to make food.

Plants and people keep each other alive. Trees give off air that we breathe in. Trees take in air that we breathe out.

How will you build your tree house without hurting your tree?

◆ Trees give us what we need to breathe.

◆ Insects are taking over this tree.

What Can Hurt Trees?

Insects attacked the tree above. The attackers in this picture are called tent caterpillars. They aren't the only kinds of insects that hurt trees. Sawfly, gypsy moth caterpillars, and Asian longhorned beetles attack trees as well.

Some kinds of **fungus** can hurt trees, too. One kind causes **wilt** disease in oaks.

Sometimes a tree gets so sick that it dies. How could you find out if the tree you chose for your tree house is healthy or sick?

◆ Lots of roots help a tree stay strong.

Why Do Trees Have Roots?

You don't want the tree your house is in to fall down. So it needs to be strong. A tree gets strength from its roots.

Roots also help bring water and **nutrients** into trees.

In a windstorm, what might happen to a tree with short roots?

◆ Which tree would you rather put your tree house in?

How Does a Tree Grow?

Trees are like children. They grow taller every year. Trees also grow wider.

Tree trunks of old trees are wider than tree trunks of young trees.

Look at these pictures. Which tree do you think is older? Which tree do you think would be best for a tree house? Why?

Arborist

Trees are a lot like people. They need regular trims, just like people need haircuts. Trees can also get sick or hurt. People who take care of trees are called arborists.

Arborists cut dead branches from trees. They cut away branches that could fall on power lines or roads. Arborists help trees with diseases. They use tools and chemicals to remove bad spots or branches.

◆ An arborist spends a lot of time up in trees.

Arborists help keep our trees healthy and beautiful.

A Symbol of Friendship

In 1912, Japan gave the United States 3,000 cherry trees. The cherry trees were a symbol of peace and friendship. The two countries became enemies during World War II in the 1940s. But after the war, they became friends again.

◆ Many people come from all over to see the cherry blossoms in Washington, DC.

The cherry trees are planted in Washington, DC. They bloom for two weeks every spring. Their blooms are a beautiful pink color. The city has a Cherry Blossom Festival to remember the special gift from Japan. Millions of people come to see the trees every year.

◆ General Sherman was named after the American Civil War hero, General William Sherman.

Did You Know?

The largest tree in the world is a giant sequoia nicknamed General Sherman. General Sherman stands about 275 feet (84 meters) tall. It is 36 feet (11 m) in diameter at its base. If you could lay the tree on a football field, it would be almost as long as the field. Scientists think the tree is more than 2,000 years old!

Here are some reasons why each tree might be a good choice. These are called pros. Each tree also has some downsides, called cons. A good tree for a tree house should be strong, with a good shape.

Choice 1: Oak Tree

Pros: An oak tree is stable, with strong roots to support it.

Cons: Insects sometimes attack oak trees. Acorns fall from some oak trees. Falling acorns could make a mess. They will also make a lot of noise when they hit your roof. It might be too loud to sleep!

Choice 2: Willow Tree

Pros: Willow trees have long leaves that are pretty and can hide your house.

Cons: Willow trees have bendy branches that might not support a tree house.

Choice 3: Maple Tree

Pros: Maple trees are strong and have long roots to support them.

Cons: Asian longhorned beetles attack maple trees. If they live in your tree, they may weaken it.

Choice 4: Pine Tree

Pros: Pine trees keep their needles all year long. That would give you some privacy.

Cons: Pines make sticky sap. That could make life a little messy.

Have you decided what tree you will build your tree house in?

Beyond the Puzzle

You chose your tree and built your tree house. You like it and want to stay and live there.

Does your plan to stay a long time change which tree you choose? Would you want to build in a young tree or an old tree? Where in the world would you like your tree to be?

Draw a picture of your perfect tree. Draw your perfect tree house in the branches. What makes your new home so great? As you have learned, there are worlds within leaves. Now you are part of those worlds.

Glossary

fungus: organisms, such as mushrooms, molds, and yeasts, that feed on organic, or living, matter.

needles: narrow leaves.

nutrients: substances living things need for life.

roots: the parts of the plant that are usually under the ground and bring water and food to the rest of the plant.

wilt: a disease in plants caused by fungi, bacteria, and other organisms.

Further Reading

Daniels, Patricia. 2017. *Trees*. Washington, DC: National Geographic Kids.

KidCrave. 2018. "Must See Treehouses for Kids." Toys and Games for Kids. https://kidcrave.com/toys-and-games/kids/must-see-treehouses/.

Pearson, Carrie A. 2018. *Stretch to the Sun: From a Tiny Sprout to the Tallest Tree on Earth*. Watertown, Mass.: Charlesbridge.

Science for Kids. 2018. "Why Leaves Change Color." Science for Kids Club. http://www.scienceforkidsclub.com/leaves-change-color.html

Additional Notes

The page references below provide answers to questions asked throughout the book. Questions whose answers will vary are not addressed.

Page 8: They grow in soil, they are tall, and they have bark.

Page 10: Children might answer that leaves fall from some trees because of wind or cold. In fact, trees shed leaves because they are not needed for food production during the winter months.

Page 11: They could damage cars and other things, hurt people and animals, and be dangerous to walk on.

Page 13: Look for galls, insects and insect damage, and fungus.

Page 14: It might fall over.

Index

acorns, 11, 19

air, 12

arborists, 16

birches, 10

branches, 4, 7, 8, 9, 16, 20, 21

fir, 10

food, 12

fruits, 7, 11

General Sherman (tree), 18

leaves, 4, 8, 9, 10, 20, 21

maple, 6, 7, 9, 10, 20

needles, 10, 20

nuts, 7, 11

oak, 6, 9, 10, 11, 13, 19

pine, 6, 7, 10, 20

plants, 4, 12

roots, 8, 14, 19, 20

spruce, 10

sunlight, 12

trunks, 8, 15

water, 14

willow, 6, 9, 10, 20